Organizing Emotions

written by
Amy Tiare

illustrated by
Sonnet Nichelle

TELEMACHUS PRESS

Cover and interior art by Sonnet Nichelle

Publishing Services by Telemachus Press, LLC
7652 Sawmill Road, Suite 304
Dublin, Ohio 43016
http://www.telemachuspress.com

ISBN: 978-1-956867-28-2 (eBook)
ISBN: 978-1-956867-29-9 (Paperback)

SELF HELP / Emotions

Version 2022.05.03

For Mom
who always believed in me

Acknowledgements

A special thank you to Jennifer Darling, my sister and owner of Transformational Healing Center, for all of her support over the years and for helping with making this book a reality.

Table of Contents

Overview

Everyone feels emotions. They are a normal part of life. However, sometimes it can be difficult to know how to process what we feel. Sometimes we push our emotions down deep inside so we don't have to deal with them. Sometimes we let them out in explosive ways that hurt the people around us. If emotions are left unprocessed in the body for long periods of time, they can affect our sleep and our physical health. If emotions are expressed in explosive ways, they can affect our relationships and our feelings of self-worth. It is important to learn how to process our emotions in a healthy way.

Having an understanding of how emotions process can help. According to Chinese medicine, the emotions we experience are associated with specific organs in the body. In order for these emotions to process, they need to be in the correct organ. When the body gets out of balance, due to stress or illness, the emotions can migrate to the wrong parts of the body. This leads to further imbalances and can start to affect our health. As we become more aware of how the body works and where everything belongs, we can help our bodies to

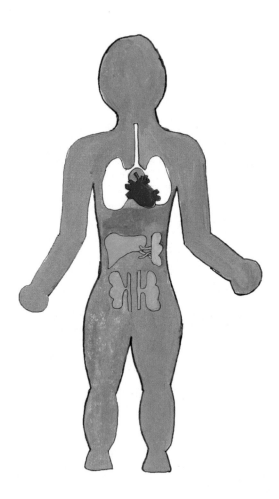

process our emotions more effectively, leading to greater harmony and balance.

The following pages contain exercises to help with organizing the emotions in the body. Use the illustrations to help create a picture in your mind of what the emotions may look like. Our minds are very powerful and can be used as a tool to achieve a greater sense of well-being. As you read through each page, take slow, deep breaths as you follow the instructions for processing each emotion. Slow, deep breaths enhance our ability to process emotions. As you breathe, your lower belly should rise and fall with each breath. If it helps, you can lie on your back and place a stuffed animal or book on your belly. If it rises and falls with each breath, then you are doing it right!

Whether you are reading this book yourself or whether someone is reading it to you, grab a blanket, get comfy, and let's process some emotions!

Grief

The lungs are located in the upper chest and are responsible for processing grief. Grief is often associated with death or a loss, such as the end of a marriage or friendship, or the loss of an opportunity. Grief often feels heavy in the chest, making it hard to breathe. Sometimes a person feeling grief will feel like crying all the time or they may shut off their emotions all together so they feel nothing. Grief can consume a person, making it hard to function in life.

Place your hands on your upper chest and take some slow, deep breaths. In your mind, as you breathe slowly, ask that all grief that may be stored, hidden, or trapped anywhere in your body be moved to your lungs to be processed, released, and let go. Move all grief to the lungs. Take several more deep breaths and imagine that there is a drainage hose going from your lungs down to the earth. All of the grief flows through this tube, like water running through a hose. The grief flows freely and completely out the hose and into the earth to be recycled.

As the grief leaves the body and flows into the earth to be recycled, bring the vibration of connection and love into your body. Replace grief with the vibration of connection and love.

Visualize your lungs filling with pure, healing light. See it healing all pain and hurt, allowing you to connect with others on a deeper level than you have in the past. Fill the lungs with connection and love.

Anxiety

The spleen is located on the left side of your body under your ribcage and is responsible for processing anxiety. Anxiety feels like having excess energy, nervousness, "butterflies" in the stomach, panic, or a feeling of impending doom. An anxious person might not be able to hold still, always tapping their feet or wringing their hands. They may be constantly looking over their shoulder thinking someone or something is there. Anxiety can greatly increase when in crowds or in new situations.

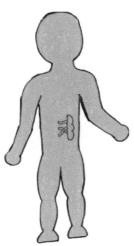

Place your hands on the left side of your torso under your ribcage and take some slow, deep breaths. In your mind, as you breathe slowly, ask that all anxiety that may be stored, hidden, or trapped anywhere in your body be moved to your spleen to be processed, released, and let go. Move all anxiety to the spleen. Take several more deep breaths and imagine that there is a drainage hose going from your spleen down to the earth. All of the anxiety flows through this tube, like water running through a hose. The anxiety flows freely and completely out the hose and into the earth to be recycled.

As the anxiety leaves the body and flows into the earth to be recycled, bring the vibration of stability and trust into your body. Replace anxiety with the vibration of stability and trust.

Visualize your spleen filling with pure, healing light. See it healing all pain and hurt, allowing you to trust on a deeper level than you have in the past. Fill the spleen with stability and trust.

Sadness

The heart is located in your chest slightly to the left side and is responsible for processing sadness. Sadness feels like being unhappy, of feeling "down," or not content. Sadness often comes when a person is disappointed or things don't go the way they expected or wanted them to go. Sadness can make it hard to be in the moment and see the good that is happening.

Place your hands on the left side of your chest and take some slow, deep breaths. In your mind, as you breathe slowly, ask that all sadness that may be stored, hidden, or trapped anywhere in your body be moved to your heart to be processed, released, and let go. Move all sadness to the heart. Take several more deep breaths and imagine that there is a drainage hose going from your heart down to the earth. All of the sadness flows through this tube, like water running through a hose. The sadness flows freely and completely out the hose and into the earth to be recycled.

As the sadness leaves the body and flows into the earth to be recycled, bring the vibration of joy and faith into your body. Replace sadness with the vibration of joy and faith.

Visualize your heart filling with pure, healing light. See it healing all pain and hurt, allowing you to feel happy on a deeper level than you have in the past. Fill the heart with joy and faith.

Fear

The kidneys are located in your lower back, about in line with your elbows when your arms are by your sides, and are responsible for processing fear. Fear feels like wanting to pull away or get away. Fear can cause the heart to race and can cause you to breathe deeper on the inbreath and shorter on the outbreath. Fear can keep a person stuck in their negative patterns and from fully enjoying life.

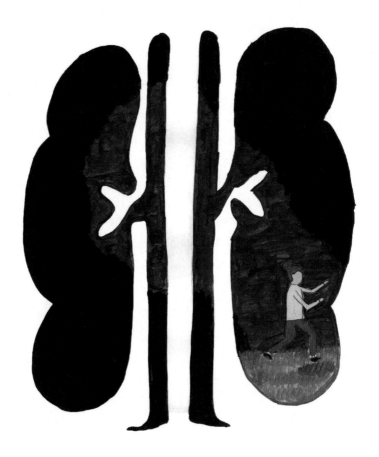

Place your hands on the lower back and take some slow, deep breaths. In your mind, as you breathe slowly, ask that all fear that may be stored, hidden, or trapped anywhere in your body be moved to your kidneys to be processed, released, and let go. Move all fear to the kidneys. Take several more deep breaths and imagine that there is a drainage hose going from your kidneys down to the earth. All of the fear flows through this tube, like water running through a hose. The fear flows freely and completely out the hose and into the earth to be recycled.

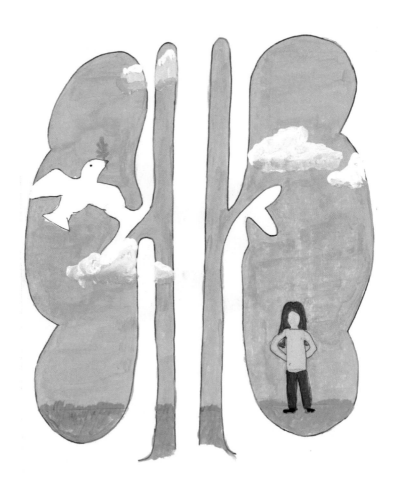

As the fear leaves the body and flows into the earth to be recycled, bring in the vibration of peace and confidence into your body. Replace fear with the vibration of peace and confidence.

Visualize your kidneys filling with pure, healing light. See it healing all pain and hurt, allowing you to be calm on a deeper level than you have in the past. Fill the kidneys with peace and confidence.

Anger

The liver is located on the right side of your body under your ribcage and is responsible for processing anger. Anger feels like aggression, tightness in the muscles, or holding the breath. A person feeling angry may get hot, the heart might pound, and the fists might clench. Anger has the potential to hurt the people around you and if turned inward, can become depression.

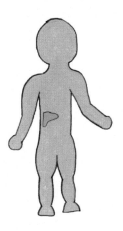

Place your hands on the right side of your torso under your ribcage and take some slow, deep breaths. In your mind, as you breathe slowly, ask that all anger that may be stored, hidden, or trapped anywhere in your body be moved to your liver to be processed, released, and let go. Move all anger to the liver. Take several more deep breaths and imagine that there is a drainage hose going from your liver down to the earth. All of the anger flows through this tube, like water running through a hose. The anger flows freely and completely out the hose and into the earth to be recycled.

As the anger leaves the body and flows into the earth to be recycled, bring in the vibration of contentment and forgiveness into your body. Replace anger with the vibration of contentment and forgiveness.

Visualize your liver filling with pure, healing light. See it healing all pain and hurt, allowing you to be you on a deeper level than you have in the past. Fill the liver with contentment and forgiveness.

Moving Forward

Now that your emotions have been moved to the correct place, have started processing, and positive energy is flowing in each organ, take a moment to notice how you feel in your body. Take several slow, deep breaths. Do you feel different now compared to when you began?

Whenever you feel strong emotions in your body you can use the practices in this book to help to calm those strong emotions down. You can do all of the emotions in one sitting or just choose the one emotion that you are struggling with the most. Most of all, remember to breathe.

About the Author

Amy Tiare grew up in a small, remote town in Alaska where she was exposed to many different types of alternative healing. These practices helped shape her way of thinking, as well as shaping her future.

At the age of 19, Amy became a massage therapist and has spent her entire adult life working to help relieve the suffering and pains that are common. Much of her time has been dedicated to self-care education, which provides people with empowerment tools that help them overcome their challenges, whether they be physical, mental, emotional, or spiritual.

Amy has helped countless clients and students develop these skills over the years. It is her desire to expand her sphere of influence by taking these powerful tools and turning them into books. Her hope is that every person throughout the world can become aware of their own bodies, emotions, and, more importantly, that they will have the tools to be able to heal, grow, and become the best they can be.

Amy currently lives in Southeastern Indiana where she practices massage therapy and craniosacral therapy. She also writes visualizations and teaches classes.

About the Illustrator

Sonnet NIchelle grew up in rural Indiana where she developed a great love for going on walks, playing the clarinet and harp, and hanging out with her friends. At a very young age, she also discovered a love of art. Although her creativity knows few bounds, the mediums she most enjoys are paint and clay. Throughout the years she has found that art provides a way to express the things that are often hard to put into words.

Sonnet also has a great love for inspirational quotes. She shares them daily on social media and is known for spreading positive vibes to the world around her. She regularly combines her love of quotes and her love of art in the gifts she makes for others.

Sonnet currently lives in Northern Idaho where she is attending the University of Idaho.

About Transformational Healing Center

Amy Tiare is an integral part of the roots of Transformational Healing Center Inc, based in Batesville, Indiana. Her skills and intuition add to their mission of helping people reach their full potential through Holistic Healthcare, including Nutritional Therapy, Acupuncture, Massage, Cupping, Craniosacral Therapy, Healing Touch, and Body Balancing.

Their staff works with people of all ages and stages of life to clear away physical, mental and emotional blocks and barriers to healing. Clearing these blocks maximizes the body's innate healing ability and leads to greater health and happiness. As people experience greater health, they are able to experience great transformations in their lives.

To learn more about our clinic, please visit:
www.transformationalhealingcenter.org

For informational video visit:
Welcome to the Transformational Healing Center

Made in the USA
Monee, IL
18 February 2023

28164389R00031